How to Make
Storybooks

Written and illustrated by Ros Asquith

Photographs by Sally Smallwood

Contents

Ideas   2

Planning   6

Writing   11

Editing   12

Illustrating   14

Covers   16

Making   18

Enjoying   21

A flow chart   22

Collins

Ideas

First you need a good idea for your story.

Will it be a funny story?

Will it be a sad story?

Will it be a story
about dogs?

Will it be a story
about cats?

Will it be about sport,
dancing or music?

3

Maybe it will be an adventure story . . .

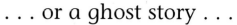

4

. . . or a detective story?

Perhaps it will be funny *and* sad *and* sporty *and* scary!

Planning

When you have your idea, you can start to plan your story.

1. Make a list of the characters who will be in your book. The characters could be animals, pirates, aliens – or they could be you and your friends. It's your choice.

2. Make a list of the things that will happen to them.

CATS R US

Take me to your reader.

3. Think of a really good way to start your story.
4. Then think of a really good ending.

5. Then work out the bits in-between. You can change your beginning and your ending later, if you want to.

9

6. Make up a good title for the book so that other people will want to read it.

Writing

Now you can start writing your story.
Don't worry about making mistakes.
What's important is the story you
have to tell.
You can write it out again later,
or type it on the computer.
If you change your mind about
anything, you can.

It's *your* story!

I must remember the "ea" in treasure!

Editing

When you have finished your story,
read it all the way through.
Do you think it's good?

1. If not, make some changes to it.
    This is called *editing* your story.

2. Ask someone else
   to read your story.
   Do they think it is good?

3. Make some more changes.
4. Ask someone else to check
   your spellings, or use a dictionary
   and check them yourself.

Illustrating

Do you want some pictures to go with your story?

You can ask a friend to do them.

Then you can do the pictures for *their* story – swap!

Or you can do your own – it's up to you.

Zig was an alien. He had a green body and purple hair.

Now you have your story and your pictures.

Covers

What you need next is a good cover. This is very important if you want other children to pick up your storybook and read it.

1. Write the title of your book on the front cover. Then put your name as the author.

2. On the back cover you should write something about the book. This is called a *blurb*.

Making

When everything is ready, you can make your story into a storybook.

fold card

join with

sticky tape

You could make it into a zig-zag book . . .

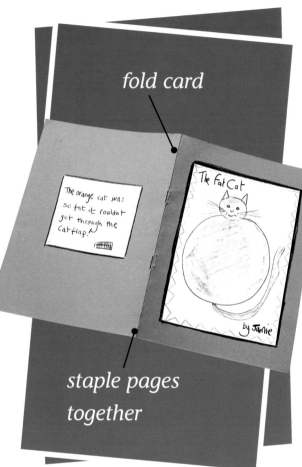

fold card

staple pages together

a stapled book . . .

Sew pages together using a needle and thick wool.

fold card

Cut out the shape after the book has been stapled or sewn.

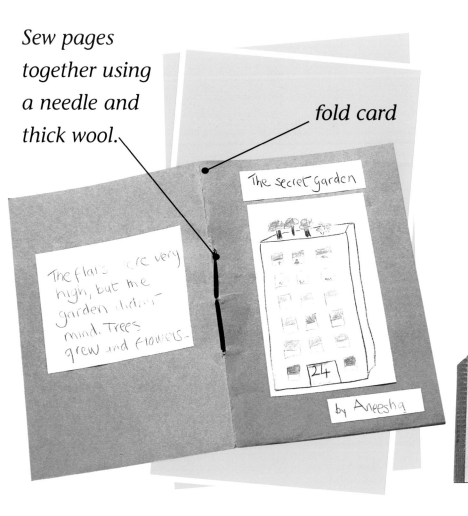

The secret garden

The flats were very high, but the garden didn't mind. Trees grew and flowers.

24

by Aneesha

The Hungry Shark

by Ashok

Spaceman

by Emma

a sewn book,

or even a funny-shaped book.

Your teacher may help you to glue
your story into
a Big Book.

Enjoying

Now it's storytime – enjoy!

A flow chart

Ideas

Enjoying

Making

Characters:
1. Teddy
2. Horse
3. Monster
Story:
Teddy and Horse find treasure but there is a monster guarding it.

Planning

Writing

Editing

Illustrating

Covers

Ideas for guided reading

Learning objectives: locate parts of the text that give particular information; use a contents page; read simple written instructions; skim-read a text to speculate what it may be about; use language to support the use of diagrams and displays when explaining.

Curriculum links: Design & Technology: making a storybook; ICT: Writing stories: communicating information using text

Interest words: adventure, ghost, detective, pirates, aliens, editing, blurb

Word count: 444

Getting started

This book may be read over two sessions.

- Show the children the book cover and ask them what they think the purpose of the book is.

- Ask the children to skim-read the book. Ask them what is happening on each page, and point out that this is an instruction book. Ask them to point out interesting and new words, e.g. *adventure, ghost, detective, aliens, editing*.

- Model how to use the contents page (p1) to find different parts of the book. Then ask the children to find the section on illustrating the book.

Reading and responding

- Ask the children to read the book independently and silently up to p21 (including text in cartoons, captions and labels as well as the main text).

- Observe each child read a short passage aloud, prompting and praising for fluency, self-correction and tackling challenging words.

- In pairs, ask the children to look at the flow chart on pp22–23 and recap the stages of making a storybook.

- Discuss with the children how well the book